EXPERIMENTS WITH FOODS

A TRUE BOOK®

by
Salvatore Tocci

Children's Press®
A Division of Scholastic Inc.

New York Toronto London Auckland Sydney
Mexico City New Delhi Hong Kong
Danbury, Connecticut

Baking a cake is like performing a science experiment.

Reading Consultant
Susan Virgilio

Science Consultant
Tenley Andrews

The photograph on the cover shows a variety of fruits and vegetables. The photograph on the title page shows a grocery cart full of foods.

The author and publisher are not responsible for injuries or accidents that occur during or from any experiments. Experiments should be conducted in the presence of or with the help of an adult. Any instructions of the experiments that require the use of sharp, hot, or other unsafe items should be conducted by or with the help of an adult.

Library of Congress Cataloging-in-Publication Data

Tocci, Salvatore.
    Experiments with foods / Salvatore Tocci.
        p. cm. (A True book)
Includes index.
Summary: Explores the science behind foods through simple experiments using everyday objects.
    ISBN 0-516-22787-4 (lib. bdg.)   0-516-27806-1 (pbk.)
    1. Cookery—Juvenile literature. 2. Science—Experiments—Juvenile literature. [1. Food—Experiments. 2. Science—Experiments. 3. Experiments.] I. Title. II. Series: True book.
TX652.5.T63 2003
507.8—dc21

                                        2003004737

CHILDREN'S PRESS, and A TRUE BOOK®, and associated logos are trademarks and or registered trademarks of Scholastic Library Publishing. SCHOLASTIC and associated logos are trademarks and or registered trademarks of Scholastic Inc.
1 2 3 4 5 6 7 8 9 10 R 12 11 10 09 08 07 06 05 04 03

Contents

A scientist often mixes chemicals in a laboratory. Some of these chemicals are used by cooks to prepare meals.

Do You Like to Cook?

Have you ever cooked any food? Perhaps you like to toast marshmallows over a campfire. Maybe you help make pancakes for breakfast or cake for a birthday celebration. If you like to eat outdoors, then perhaps you help grill the hot dogs or hamburgers on the barbecue.

Whenever you help prepare a meal, you may think of yourself as a cook. Actually, anyone who prepares a meal can also be considered a scientist. Some of the ingredients a cook uses are actually chemicals that can be found in a science laboratory. Just as a scientist experiments in a lab, a cook may experiment in a kitchen to come up with a new recipe. Here is your chance to experiment with foods to learn more about science.

What's in Your Kitchen Cabinets?

Your kitchen is like a science laboratory. The cabinets are filled with chemicals you can use to carry out some interesting experiments. One of these chemicals is sodium bicarbonate, which is commonly called baking soda. Find out why

The ingredients in many of these food products are some of the chemicals that you can find in a science laboratory.

baking soda is an important ingredient in the batter used to make cake.

Popping Open

You will need:
- measuring cup
- white vinegar
- plastic bag you can seal without zipper lock
- paper napkin
- tablespoon
- baking soda
- twist tie
- sink

Pour a half cup of vinegar and a quarter cup of warm water into the plastic bag. Seal the bag and make sure that it does not leak. Tear the paper napkin in half. Put 2 tablespoons of baking soda in the center of the paper napkin. Bring the edges of the napkin together and wrap the twist tie around them.

Open the plastic bag halfway. Drop the napkin

Use the twist tie so that none of the baking soda spills out of the napkin.

containing the baking soda into the bag and reseal it quickly. Gently shake the bag and put it in the sink. Stand back and watch what happens.

The bag swells up and then pops open. This happens because vinegar and baking soda are two chemicals that react with each other. They react to make bubbles of carbon dioxide gas. The gas bubbles fill the plastic bag, causing it to swell and then pop open. When a cake is baking in the oven, baking soda reacts with chemicals in the batter to make these gas bubbles. These bubbles cause the cake to rise.

Try experimenting with different sizes of plastic bags, different amounts of vinegar and baking soda, and water of different temperatures. Which combination produces the biggest pop?

Baking soda causes a cake to rise as it is baked in an oven.

Baking soda is a type of chemical known as a **base.** Bases usually feel slippery, like soap. Vinegar is a type of chemical known as an **acid.** Acids usually taste sour, like grapefruit juice. An acid is mixed with baking soda to make baking powder. See how this makes baking powder act differently than baking soda.

11

Experiment 2
Making Bubbles

You will need:
- two small glasses
- labeling tape
- marker
- two teaspoons
- baking soda
- baking powder
- orange juice

Fill both glasses halfway with warm water. Label one glass "baking soda" and the other glass "baking powder." Add 1 teaspoon of baking soda to one glass and 1 teaspoon of baking powder to the other glass. Watch what happens. Do you see gas bubbles in the water containing baking powder?

When water is added, the acid and the base in the baking powder react with each other and produce gas bubbles. Baking soda

Look closely
for the tiny gas
bubbles that are
created when
baking powder is
added to water.

does not con-
tain an acid,
so there is
no chemical
reaction to
make gas
bubbles.

Rinse out both glasses. Now fill
both glasses halfway with orange juice. Again add
1 teaspoon of baking soda to one glass and 1
teaspoon of baking powder to the other glass.
What do you notice about the gas bubbles
produced this time by the baking soda?

Orange juice contains an acid. The base in baking soda reacts with the acid in the orange juice to produce gas bubbles. Remember that the baking powder already contains an acid. So when you add baking powder to the orange juice, you have much more acid than you do when you add baking soda. All of this acid causes fewer gas bubbles to be produced. In addition to making bubbles, baking soda can be used to tell the difference between an acid and a base.

Acids and bases differ in other ways besides the way they feel and taste. Learn how baking soda can be used to reveal another difference between an acid and a base.

Turning Colors

You will need:
- adult helper
- red cabbage
- sharp knife
- cutting board
- pot with lid
- stove
- clock
- strainer
- large glass jar
- tablespoon
- baking soda ✓
- measuring cup
- vinegar

Ask an adult to help you chop half a head of red cabbage into small pieces. Place the pieces in the pot and cover them with water. Put the lid on the pot and boil the red cabbage for fifteen minutes. The liquid should turn a dark purplish color. After the pot has cooled, pour the colored liquid through the strainer into the glass jar.

Add 1 tablespoon of baking soda to a half cup of water and stir for one minute. Add 3 tablespoons of the purple liquid to the water and baking soda. What color does the purple liquid turn?

Rinse the measuring cup and tablespoon. Add 1 tablespoon of vinegar to a half cup of water and stir. Add 3 tablespoons of purple liquid to the vinegar. What color do you see this time?

If a base is added to the liquid made from red cabbage, the liquid will turn green. If an acid is added, the liquid will turn red. Experiment with different ingredients and foods you have in your kitchen. You can try baking powder, sugar, salt, and the juice from a lemon. If a food does not change the color of the purple liquid, then the food is neither an acid nor a base. Anything that is not an acid or base is said to be neutral.

Experiment to see if other colored vegetables, such as broccoli and beets, produce a liquid that changes color when you add baking soda and vinegar.

Besides red cabbage, can any other vegetables or fruits be used to test for the presence of acids and bases?

What Foods Can You Make?

When people say they are going to prepare a meal, they usually use foods they buy at a supermarket. Many people, however, actually make their own foods when preparing a meal. For example, they might use the cream from milk to make butter. All you have to do to make butter is get some cream and do a whole lot of shaking.

18

Experiment 4
Shaking It Up

You will need:
- heavy cream
- plastic container with an airtight lid
- tape (optional)
- knife
- piece of bread

Pour the heavy cream into the container until the container is a little more than half full. Put the lid on the container. Make sure the lid is on tightly. If the lid does not screw on, use tape to keep it from coming off. Start shaking the container. Keep shaking until you see lumps appear in the cream. You may have to shake for twenty to thirty minutes. If your arms get tired, ask someone to shake the container while you take a break.

You can use a mixer if you want to turn the cream into butter more quickly.

Stop shaking when the lumps stop getting bigger. These lumps are butter. Open the lid and carefully pour out the remaining liquid. Spread some of the butter on the bread. How does it taste? See what other food you can make from milk, this time by heating it.

HEAVY CREAM

Turning Up the Heat

You will need:
- adult helper
- tablespoon
- buttermilk
- measuring cup
- whole milk
- small pot
- stove
- thermometer
- rennin tablet (sold under the trade name Junket)
- coffee filter
- strainer
- sink
- salt

Add 1 tablespoon of buttermilk to three-quarters of a cup of whole milk. Allow the milk to sit at room temperature for at least four hours. Ask an adult to help you warm the milk in a small pot to 85°F (29°C). Be careful not to overheat the milk. While stirring the milk, add half of the rennin tablet. Slowly increase the temperature to 100°F (38°C), but no higher.

Continue heating for several minutes. Allow the pot to cool. What has happened to the milk? Place the coffee filter inside the strainer. Slowly pour the contents of the pot through the filter and allow the liquid to drain into the sink. The liquid is called **whey**. The solid material that collects on the filter is called

curds. The curds are cheese. Some whey still remains mixed with the curds. Allow most of the whey to evaporate. Shake some salt on your cheese. How does it taste?

Scientists often apply heat to get chemicals to react with one another to make something they want. Without supplying the heat from a stove, you would not have been able to make cheese from milk. There is another food you can make from milk. However, this time you have to get the milk very cold.

Many of the cheeses sold in stores have been allowed to age for months.

Experiment 6

Lowering the Temperature

You will need:
- adult helper
- measuring cup
- sugar
- small plastic bag
- non-dairy creamer
- whole milk
- teaspoon
- vanilla
- large plastic bag
- ice cubes
- towel
- hammer
- rock salt

Place a quarter cup of sugar into the small plastic bag. Pour a half cup of the non-dairy creamer into the measuring cup. Add a half cup of whole milk and a quarter teaspoon of vanilla. Carefully pour the contents of the measuring cup into the bag containing the sugar. Seal the bag and place it inside the larger bag.

24

Make sure that you seal the small bag tightly.

Ask an adult to place ice cubes in a towel and crush them by hitting them with the hammer. Place the crushed ice in the larger bag. Add enough ice to surround the smaller bag. Add a half cup of rock salt to the ice. Seal the larger bag. Roll the larger bag back and forth on a flat surface.

Be careful not to press too hard on the larger bag or you might cause the smaller bag inside to pop open.

Continue rolling the larger bag until the contents of the smaller bag have frozen. When the contents are frozen, remove the smaller bag, open it up, and use the spoon to enjoy your ice cream. You can add nuts and chocolate syrup if you would like to.

You have to lower the temperature if you want a liquid, such as milk, to freeze. Surrounding milk with ice cubes will get it cold. However, the temperature will not get cold enough for the milk to freeze and turn into ice cream. This is why you add the rock salt to the ice cubes. The mixture of salt and ice lowers the temperature enough for the milk to turn into ice cream.

How Can You Keep Foods Fresh?

Most foods contain one or more **preservatives** to keep them fresh. Without preservatives, bread would spoil in just a few days. A green mold would start to grow on it. Refrigerators also help to keep foods fresh. If left at room temperature, eggs would spoil quickly.

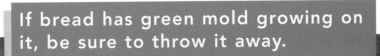

If bread has green mold growing on it, be sure to throw it away.

Before preservatives and refrigerators were available, keeping foods fresh took some work. People often added salt or vinegar to foods to prevent them from spoiling. The food was then placed in sealed containers to keep out air and moisture, which can make food spoil quickly. The next experiment will show you how you can keep some foods fresh even when they are left out in the open.

Preserving Fruit

You will need:
- adult helper
- sharp knife
- apple
- glass
- orange juice
- paper towel
- two small dishes
- clock

Ask an adult to help you cut a slice from the apple. Place the slice in a glass filled with orange juice. Wait five minutes and then pour off the juice. Blot the apple slice with a paper towel and place it on a small dish. Ask the adult to help you cut another slice from the apple. Place this slice on the other dish.

Examine the slices every five minutes. Is the slice you soaked in orange juice still white? Has the other slice started to turn brown?

Which one of these apple slices would you eat?

Oxygen in the air causes fruits to turn brown and slowly lose their freshness. Orange juice contains **vitamin C**, which can preserve fruits. Vitamin C is a **nutrient**. A nutrient is something you need in your diet to stay healthy. Vitamin C keeps the oxygen from causing the slice of apple to turn brown.

Experiment with other fruits, such as peaches and pears, to see if orange juice keeps them as fresh. Try other juices, such as apple and grape, to see if they preserve fruits as well as orange juice does. Find out another way that you can keep an apple fresh.

32

Experiment 8

Keeping Cookies Moist

You will need:
- adult helper
- sharp knife
- apple
- slice of bread
- two cookie tins or kitchen canisters
- cookie

Ask an adult to help you cut two slices from the apple. Place one apple slice and a slice of bread in one of the cookie tins or canisters. Place the other apple slice and a cookie in the other tin or canister. Cover both containers. Wait a few days and then check the contents of each container.

Did the bread get stale while the cookie stayed fresh? The apple, bread, and cookie all contain sugar.

Sugar absorbs moisture from the air. An apple has more sugar than bread does. So the apple slice absorbs more water, keeping it moist and fresh.

In summer, a bag of sugar may get hard because of all the moisture it has absorbed from the air.

But the cookie has more sugar than the apple does. So the cookie absorbs more water, keeping it moist and fresh. Which would stay freshest if you placed all three in the same container?

Even if a food is fresh, it still may not taste good. For example, have you ever eaten a tough piece of meat? To make sure that the meat is not too tough, a cook may first sprinkle some meat tenderizer on it. The next experiment will show you how the tenderizer can soften a tough piece of meat. You will also learn why you can use gelatin as a substitute for meat.

Experiment 9

Getting Softer

You will need:
- adult helper
- gelatin
- two shallow trays or baking pans
- refrigerator
- meat tenderizer
- clock
- pencil with eraser

Ask an adult to help you prepare the gelatin according to the directions on the package. Before the gelatin cools, pour equal amounts of it into two shallow trays or baking pans and place them in the refrigerator. After the gelatin has hardened, remove both trays from the refrigerator. Cover one of the trays with a thin layer of meat tenderizer. Wait about fifteen minutes. Use the eraser end of the pencil to poke the gelatin in each tray.

Use the pencil to poke the gelatin gently.

Did the meat tenderizer make the gelatin soft and watery?

Like meat, gelatin is made of mostly **protein**. Protein is one of the nutrients you need in your diet. Different proteins are used to build many parts of your body, including your muscles, hair, and skin. Various foods, such as meat and eggs, supply the proteins you need.

However, proteins can make a piece of meat tough. Meat tenderizer works by breaking down the proteins to soften the meat. By the way, fresh pineapple works just like meat tenderizer does. See for yourself by putting a fresh pineapple slice on the gelatin. Experiment with other fruits to see if they can break down proteins the same way pineapple does.

Because fresh pineapples work just like meat tenderizer, they cannot be added to gelatin desserts.

Fun With Foods

Your kitchen is a place in which you can find the ingredients and foods you need to carry out some interesting experiments. Carrying out experiments with foods is one way to learn some science. However, like most people, you probably would rather eat foods than experiment with them. You probably also like the taste of some foods more than others.

Did you ever wonder why even your favorite food has no taste when you have a cold? The following experiment will show you how important your nose is to tasting food. You will probably be surprised to find out how difficult it is to identify foods that you eat every day.

Experiment 10

Holding Your Nose

You will need:
- adult helper
- sharp knife
- various foods
- drinking glass

Have an adult prepare bite-size samples of different foods. Make sure that each sample is about the same size and shape. Check your kitchen to see what kinds of foods you can find. Foods that you can use include a sugar cube, a raw potato, an onion, cheese, nuts, chocolate, and various fruits.

> You can bite the food, but be sure to spit it out before tasting the next sample. This way you will avoid any aftertastes.

Close your eyes and pinch your nose shut. Stick out your tongue and have an adult place a sample of food on it. Chew it and say what you think the food is. Spit out the food and rinse out your mouth with water. Try another sample of food. How many did you get correct? Test your family and friends to see how well they do.

Your tongue has tiny **taste buds** on it that help you taste food. However, your nose is also important for tasting food. In fact, your nose is much more sensitive than your tongue. When you cannot smell food, such as when you have a cold, food does not taste as good.

Both your tongue and nose help you taste the foods you eat.

To Find Out More

If you would like to learn more about science projects with foods, check out these additional resources.

 **Books**

Gardner, Robert. **Science Projects About Kitchen Chemistry.** Enslow Publishers, 2002.

Hartzog, John Daniel. **Everyday Science Experiments in the Kitchen.** Power Kids Press, 2000.

Maynard, Chris. **Kitchen Science.** DK Publishing, 2001.

Pearce, Q.L. **Kid Science: Kitchen Science Experiments.** Lowell House, 1999.

Robinson, Richard. **Science Magic in the Kitchen.** Aladdin Paperbacks, 2001.

Ross, Michael Elsohn. **Kitchen Lab: You Are the Scientist.** Carolthoda Books, 2002.

VanCleave, Janice. **Janice VanCleave's Food and Nutrition for Every Kid.** John Wiley & Sons, 1999.

Organizations and Online Sites

Catch a Rainbow

*http://www.kidzone.ws/
science/rainbow/htm*

Learn how to create all the colors of a rainbow inside a bowl using food coloring and milk.

Food and Drug Administration

5600 Fishers Lane
Rockville, MD 20857-0001
888-463-6332
*http://www.fda.gov/oc/
opacom/kids*

This is the FDA Kids' home page, on which you can take a quiz on food safety.

Healthy Teeth

http://www.healthyteeth.org

Click on "Experiments and Activities." Using vinegar and eggs, you can check out how the fluoride in toothpaste protects against tooth decay. You can also perform an experiment that describes how to test the sugar content of different foods.

How Stuff Works

*http://www.howstuffworks.
com/food-preservation.htm*

This site contains information about preserving food. You can carry out an experiment using a method known as freeze-drying. Freeze-drying is most commonly used to make instant coffee, but you can test it out on apples, potatoes, or carrots.

Rising With Yeast

*http://www.cbc4kids.cbc.ca/
archives.html*

Click on "Do-It-Yourself Experiments." You can then learn the answers to questions like "Why does food spoil?" and "Why are sweet things bad for your teeth?" Then click on the "Kitchen Demo" to carry out an experiment.

Taste

*http://faculty.washington.
edu/chudler/chtaste.html*

This site contains three experiments involving taste buds.

Important Words

acid chemical that tastes sour and turns the purplish liquid from red cabbage to red

base chemical that feels slippery and turns the purplish liquid from red cabbage to green

curds solid particles in milk used to make cheese

nutrient item in the diet that helps keep a person healthy

preservatives chemicals that keep food fresh

protein nutrient in food that is used to build many body parts

taste buds tiny bumps on the tongue used to taste food

vitamin C nutrient the body needs to stay healthy that can also be used to keep fruits fresh

whey liquid or watery part of milk

46

Index

Meet the Author

Salvatore Tocci is a science writer who lives in East Hampton, New York, with his wife, Patti. He was a high school biology and chemistry teacher for almost thirty years. As a teacher, he always encouraged his students to perform experiments to learn about science. The Toccis love to cook and entertain their family and friends with Italian specialty dishes, such as osso bucco Milanese.